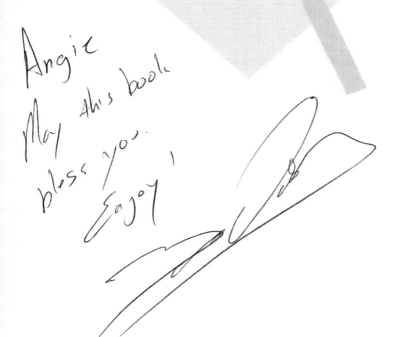

CHASING HAPPILY EVER AFTER

building blocks to a better relationship

Brian E. Wallace

Angie
May this book
bless you.
Enjoy!

CONTENTS

ACKNOWLEDGEMENTS

If I truly sat down and tried to say thank you to everyone who has had an impact in my life, I believe it would fill this entire book. That's just how many family and friends I am grateful to for their positive influence upon my life. Therefore to not bore you with too many sentiments, I want to quickly say thank you to key people that had a direct impact on the making of this book.

First and foremost I am grateful to my Lord and Savior Jesus Christ, whom not only saved me from my sins, but equipped me with the talents and guidance to share helpful insights to others. The second greatest influence upon my life, and the making of this book would be my mother. There is little she hasn't gone through to help me be successful. Thank you for being the best mom possible.

I am grateful: to my Senior Pastor Brian Kennedy who mentored me in the faith, Pastor Micheal Calloway who guided me through a very challenging time in my life, Dana Marie Booker and Dr. Christiane Stephens for editing, Dr. Leah

Fortson for consulting, Keonte McDonald for the countless hours of co-hosting SimplifyComplexity.org podcast, Harris Booker for your friendship and sponsorship of Simplify Complexity, Johnnell Williams and Leon McCrary for the many brainstorming sessions, Dana Tyler and Koria January for continually pushing me to finish, and to my entire Mt Zion Church family.

Finally, I want to say thank you to everyone who contributed and partnered with me to help fund the publishing and marketing of this book.

Thank you!

PREFACE

You might be wondering why I chose to write a book on relationships, or why I devote my time hosting a weekly relationship podcast?

On occasions, I find I ask myself these very questions. Not because I'm unsure of what I'm doing or why, but because life has a funny way of changing your plans, and God has a magnificent way of taking those detours and using them for His glory.

As one not raised in the church, I knew of God, but was far from following Him. I lived my life on my terms, and as a result made many bad choices. When it came to relationships those choices weren't any better. Heavily influenced by peers and cultural norms, I saw women as objects and sex as an objective. I didn't know it then, but I was lost when it came to understanding God's plan for relationships. I looked for love in all the wrong places, and sadly hurt people along the way.

It wasn't until I gave my heart to Christ in the year of 2000 that I began to understand what a healthy relationship was supposed to look like. I made changes for the better; I grew as a Christian and stopped having sex outside of marriage. Eventually, I met a beautiful woman who was also new to her faith. It was an exciting time! Our relationship quickly progressed to marriage, and I felt like I was living the dream… that is, until I wasn't.

There are two major reasons why I'm writing this book. The first has to do with my calling. The second has to do with a burden for relationships.

When you talk about a person's calling, it's important to understand where God has called them from, but it's also important to understand where God has called them to. God equips us with gifts and talents to live out our purpose. One of the gifts I've been given is the ability to teach. I've dedicated my life to sharing God's Word with others and taking my experiences to help people better understand God's desire for them.

Though my calling may explain why I teach God's word; it doesn't fully explain why I am sensitive to relationships. To grasp this, it helps to understand a "ministry burden." A burden is not always a bad thing. In this case, it's something that weighs heavy on your heart and moves you to go above and beyond to help others. Sometimes people choose the ministry burdens they want to carry. Other times those burdens are placed upon them out of life circumstances, as is the case for me.

My burden for relationships was birthed out of one of the most challenging times in my life, my divorce. I don't think words can express how much I hate that word. Every time I say it, I feel disgusted. Every time I hear couples mention the idea, I want to help them avoid its destruction.

Divorce wasn't something that I chose. I tried my best, to be the best husband I could possibly be. That doesn't mean I did everything right. You don't have a breakdown in marriage and not have a role in it.

What it does mean is that I have my integrity, but unfortunately that doesn't always make you feel better. It doesn't make the pain go away. It doesn't stop people from judging you. It doesn't stop you from judging yourself.

There were times I really struggled to move forward in ministry, times, that I questioned God, and asked why me? But I came to the realization that my past is a powerful testimony of learning, forgiving, picking up the pieces, and building again. God wants to use our experiences to help others. It is through our weaknesses that God is glorified (2Cor. 12:9).

Not only do I better understand relationships from the life I lived before becoming a Christian, but I've also come to understand the challenges many Christians face as they seek to do things God's way. There is a false sense of security that says you simply need to abstain from sexual impurity and marry a believer and then, POOF, you'll have a godly, lasting marriage. WRONG! It is a beginning, but far from the end.

My desire is to be an agent of change, and to help others avoid the pitfalls of relationships. There are many people who want to do things God's way, but getting there can be a rollercoaster. This book is a modern Christian guide to the relationship process. It asks the tough questions like, what is God's desire for me in singleness, or while dating? Is happiness even possible if I choose to remain single? How does dating translate to and impact marriage? How does one stay married?

Understanding the big picture to the relationship process is like having blueprints to a structure you are building. Although, you will still labor through the process, you will know the steps to take to make the right choices to complete the building.

Whether single, dating, courting, or married, everyone is building something. The question is what are you building; will it withstand the winds of time, the floods of negative feelings, the droughts of affection, or those angry earthquakes? In the end, how will you find happiness, and if you do, will it survive?

Introduction

Taking Aim!

How often do you think about relationships? Regardless of our relationship status, most of us have relationship desires. These desires can range from a potential partner's looks to their aspirations. Let's start by taking a moment to write some of your relationship wants.

Relationship Desires

- looks
- height
- education level
- career type
- family goals
- athletic
- romantic passions
- etc

MY RELATIONSHIP DESIRES?

Wanting the prize

Have you ever gone to a carnival and seen some of the tantalizing prizes offered? People love winning those prizes and will pay money to win. Consider the ping-pong toss game as an example. In this game, there are small cups floating in a pool; the object is to throw a ping-pong ball from a distance and land it inside the cup. This may seem easy, but if you've ever played this game, or any carnival game, they can be far from easy.

Imagine for a moment, you pay five dollars for five ping-pong balls. After missing all five attempts, you felt really close to winning, so you purchase ten more. Attempt, after attempt, you get closer and closer, but before you know it, you've spent a hundred dollars, and walk away empty-handed. How do you feel?

If you've ever lost money on these games, then you may have felt as I have: frustrated, disappointed, and even hurt. Some people walk away so annoyed they vow to never play a carnival game again. Why? Because of the disappointment of losing! The average person won't pay a hundred dollars knowing they will lose! Deep down, those who are willing to sacrifice and play **believe winning is possible.**

A question I would like to present to you is this, how many people are walking away from relationships feeling frustrated and hurt, vowing to never love again? Similar to the example above, those who are willing to sacrifice their hearts in relationships believe a winning relationship is possible.

When people date, they have high hopes that their special someone is "thee One." When people get married there's a belief they will beat the odds. They want the prize of a good marriage. They want the storybook ending!

You know... The story, where the guy finds the girl, and the girl gets the guy... they fall in love at first sight, and ride off into the sunset. Yeah, that story! The one that ends *Happily Ever After*.

Unfortunately, for many, that story is not ending happily

According to the American Psychological Association almost fifty percent of all marriages end in divorce.[1] That's not a happy ending! The average person doesn't think about divorce as they walk down the aisle. Furthermore, disappointments in relationships are not limited to just divorce.

When people fantasize about sex, their fantasies don't include getting sexually transmitted diseases, yet, it happens! Almost forty-five percent of all sexually active Americans will contract genital herpes.[2]

Did you know only one in thirty people wait to have sex until marriage? Eight out of ten teen fathers don't stick around to marry the mother of their child, and forty-one percent of married couples experience infidelity.[3]

People in love don't expect to be cheated on or to raise their children alone. Yet, it has become the norm within relationships. Where are the *Happily Ever After* stories?

I mention these points only to highlight some of the challenges facing relationships today. People want the prize of a successful relationship, but the current process is leading to more disappointments rather than triumphs. Should we keep doing the same thing? No, that would be insane! Instead of giving up on relationships, I think we should try a different approach.

SOMETHING DIFFERENT

Let's go back to the ping-pong toss game for a moment. I remember one day while at an amusement park, watching person after person purchase ping-pong balls, aim for the cups, only for them to bounce out and lose. That is until I saw something different. In this particular case an individual took their ping-pong ball and bounced it off the ground in front of the cups. As odd as this appeared, amazingly after a couple of tries and finding the right angle, they won.

In that moment the light bulb went off in my head. Everyone else only saw one approach, aiming directly for the cups. Unfortunately, the velocity caused the ball to bounce out. By taking a different approach and aiming at the ground it allowed the ball to ricochet off the ground, changing its velocity, and landing softer in the cup.

Could it be there is a different approach to relationships?

Why do people choose to follow the same destructive patterns time and time again? You would think those who marry for a second time, would do things different. Yet, statistics show a second marriage is more likely to fail than the first, and the third is even more likely to fail than the second! Talk about the definition of insanity.

In part, there's a false assumption that one should innately know how to pick the right mate, build a great marriage, and live *Happily Ever After*. Yet, where does that assumption originate? Most people don't take relationship courses in school. How many can honestly observe their parents as the best example? Truthfully, the average person doesn't even seek relationship advice until they're in relationship trouble.

Consider for a moment you travel through time to gain relationship advice from your younger-self or older-self. Who would you rather talk to? How would their advice differ? Most likely your younger-self would tell you to follow your heart, and go where it leads you. Whereas, your older-self, after experiencing heartache, would likely tell you to make different choices; wiser choices as to whom you give your heart to. Ultimately sharing a different approach.

🖤 Getting there

There is a famous quote by Zig Ziglar, *"If you aim at nothing; you will hit it every time."* Think about the relationship desires you wrote down earlier.

What is your aim to get there? Which self (younger or older) will you listen to?

Before you enter into a relationship, what is your objective? If you're single, what is your preparation? If dating, what is your purpose? If physically intimate, what are your boundaries? If married and your love begins to fade, what is your solution? These simple questions can make all the difference between failure and success.

> IF YOU
> AIM AT
> NOTHING;
> YOU WILL
> HIT IT
> EVERY
> TIME
> ~ ZIG ZIGLAR

Jesus made a powerful statement I want you to examine.

"For which of you, intending to build a tower, does not sit down first and count the cost, whether he has enough to finish it lest, after he has laid the foundation, and is not able to finish, all who see it begin to mock him, saying, "This man began to build and was not able to finish" (Luke 14:28-30).

Replace the word "tower" in Luke 14:28 with the word "marriage." For which of you, intending to build a marriage, does not sit down first and count the cost? In this analogy Jesus helps us to understand that good intentions are not enough, building something takes more than desire.

> **Desire doesn't always produce results.**

Life shows us that people have many desires. Desires to be financially secure, to earn a college education, to have a good paying job, or move into a nice home. These things are obtainable, yet not everyone who wants them will obtain them. Why? Because desire doesn't always produce results. The same is true for relationships. Having a happy marriage requires more than desire, it requires counting the cost.

Counting the cost in relationships means understanding and making the critical choices necessary to be successful. Choices that require both sacrifice and thought. Choices that are not always romantic or fun.

Have people truly thought about what it will cost to fall in love with the right person, or what sacrifices must be made to have a lasting marriage?

From this point forward, it is time to do things different. No matter where you are in the relationship process (single, dating, courting, or married), success is

> **Have you truly considered what is required of you to have a lasting marriage?**

not an accident. It is something you work at and build towards.

WHAT SACRIFICES ARE YOU WILLING TO MAKE IN
RELATIONSHIPS?

Building a solid relationship

Building a solid relationship is similar to building a solid home. In
both instances there are several stages that must be completed
correctly before moving to the next stage. Each stage adds its own
value to the completion of the home. You don't build the frame
before you lay the foundation, and you don't move in before you
install the roof. Skipping a stage or leaving a stage incomplete
compromises the structural integrity
of a home.

Similarly, skipping or failing to
complete steps will compromise the
integrity of a relationship. Building
a solid relationship is a process.
There are stages and building takes
time. The choices you make when single impact the people you
date, and the spouse you'll become. The habits you create while

courting shape the habits you will repeat during marriage.

As much as we would love to hit an "easy button" there just isn't one. There is no magic wand, fairy godmother, or glass slipper. A *Happily Ever After* isn't something that "just happens."

In the next five chapters I will share a different approach to achieve better results. We'll compare five stages of building a home, to five stages of building a solid relationship. There will be some familiar approaches to watch for, but some will be challenging and unfamiliar.

To DO different, you have to THINK different

- If you are tired of getting the same results from relationships, then this is for you.

- If you want to seek God's will within relationships, then this is for you too.

- If you want your *Happily Ever After*, keep reading, this is definitely for you.

It's time to count the costs, understand what it takes to get there, and take aim!

SMALL WINS ARE A STEADY APPLICATION
OF SMALL ADVANTAGES
-- CHARLES DUHIGG

1

The Foundation
DISCIPLESHIP IN CHRIST

The foundation is the most important part of any structure. It's what provides stability and determines what you are building. If the foundation of a structure is weak, everything that sits on it will be weak.

There is no difference when it comes to relationships. The relationships you build will depend on the foundation you start with.

When working on your foundation, the focus is not on the other person, who they are, what they did, or what they need to do. It has nothing to do with them, but instead, everything to do with you and God.

In this stage, we will put emphasis on your relationship with God. This is important, so that you are strong enough to support the needs of a relationship. To do this, you will need to surrender control to God. The biggest challenge in doing what God asks is getting out of His way; if you don't, you will sabotage your *Happily Ever After* faster than you ever thought possible.

If already married, don't dare assume the foundational stage doesn't apply to you. Too many couples work on surface issues before working on the deeply rooted ones. It makes no sense to patch a crack in the wall before fixing the crack in the foundation. Fixing the wall would only be temporary. The same goes for couples who try to fix their relationship when their foundation in Christ is faulty.

> Seek a long-term solution, rather than a short-term fix.

If you're single, take advantage of your singleness! This is the easiest and most opportune time to work on foundational principals. Even if you are currently dating, slow things down and get your foundation right!

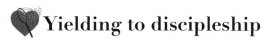 Yielding to discipleship

IN YOUR OWN WORDS DESCRIBE DISCIPLESHIP?

> SALVATION IS FREE, BUT DISCIPLESHIP COSTS EVERYTHING WE HAVE.
>
> - BILLY GRAHAM

Recent surveys show, that while most American's are professing to be Christians, they struggle to understand key components of their faith. Over eighty percent of Americans own a bible, but only eleven percent of them have read the Bible.[4] How can a person successfully live out their faith if they don't understand it? Imagine an NBA player who doesn't know what traveling means, or a ballerina who can't pirouette. It's unlikely to experience success without foundational principles. Similarly, a Christian who does not know their faith will find it difficult to build a successful relationship with Christ.

> *"I am the vine; you are the branches. If you remain in me and I in you, you will bear much fruit; a apart from me you can do nothing" (John 15:5).*

The analogy that Jesus provides above refers to a grapevine producing grapes. If a branch is disconnected from the vine it will no longer get the nutrients it needs to produce fruit. Eventually, the branch will dry up and wither.

Living a godly life, and approaching relationships in a godly manner isn't always easy. The nutrients you need to sustain your effort doesn't come from you; it comes from God. God is the substance of life and the source of your strength.

A key for Christians to learn and grow in their faith is through systematic discipleship. Systematic discipleship is more than just going to church on Sundays. It is a process where you submit yourself to Christ, His teachings, and to spiritual mentorship to be transformed into the image of Christ.

> PROCESS: While salvation can happen in a moment, discipleship doesn't happen overnight. Learning and growing in your faith takes time, therefore, don't look to rush through the process.

> SUBMISSION: The act of yielding to authority. When you commit your life to Christ you are surrendering to Him. No longer is the emphasis about what you want, but rather what God wants for you.

> TEACHING: You're not just yielding to the person of Christ, but also to His teachings. Jesus said it plainly. "If

you love me, you will keep my commandments (John 14:15)." Christ's commandments are His instructions to us that we may live a productive life. A life of obedience characterizes those who choose to follow Jesus.

MENTORSHIP: God instituted the church to accomplish His great commission, "Go therefore and make disciples of all the nations" (Matt. 28:19). Not only are you to be discipled, but you are to disciple others. The body of Christ (believers) is meant to help one another grow in their faith.

TRANSFORMATION: When your life becomes impacted by the power of Christ, you will not be the same. Your life and the way you live, love, and date will be different. Paul Washer said it best, "How is it possible for a pedestrian to be hit by a truck going 50 mph and not show signs of a collision? It's not possible!"

THE CHRIST-DIRECTED LIFE
CHRIST is on the throne
Self is yielding to Christ
Interests are directed by Christ, resulting in harmony with God's plan

Discipleship is such an important step that if you are single, you shouldn't consider a relationship until you have been discipled. If you are dating, you need discipleship before you get married, and if you are married, the impact of discipleship is equally important because it affects the way you live together no matter the state of your marriage.

This may sound unreasonable, but that's how important discipleship is in a relationship. It impacts the very essence of who you are and how you live. Take time to be a disciple of Christ. Through this process, you will gain insights that will help you become a better mate. **Consider why you do the things you do?**

Gaining Christ-centered values

Why does a person choose to forgive someone even though they don't seem to be deserving of forgiveness? Why wait to have sex until marriage, or stay in a difficult marriage to work things out?

WHAT IS YOUR "WHY" IN "WHAT" YOU DO?

The process of discipleship helps to shape your values. This is your "why," in "what" you do. I'm referring to your actions and convictions. Let's take love for example; for some, love is a response based on how others meet their needs. I love you *because* of what you can do for me. I love you *because* of how you make me feel, or I love you *because* of the way you look. Worldly love revolves around selfishness, it's a *because* type of love. At the root, it's all about self.

However, Christ teaches that true love, agape love is sacrificial. Pledging love is a responsibility, and with this, we strive to meet needs unconditionally. I love you *even though* you get on my nerves at times, or *even though* you've gained extra weight. An *even though* type of love is how God wants you to love your mate or spouse.

What does this tell us? Even the simplicities of how you love are a result of your foundation. God brings purpose to what you do, and how you do it. If you are doing something with a lack of understanding, then what you're doing won't last. This is how some people can sincerely make commitments, but in time, break them. The original commitment lacked understanding of what that meant, which could be related to tradition, peer pressure, or something else. As a result, challenges become too difficult to sustain their commitment.

SOMETHING TO THINK ABOUT

Expect your values in relationships to be challenged: These are the winds of temptations, the quakes of anger, and the storms of despair trying to break you!

What have you allowed within your past to negotiate your values? Why?

Moving forward what will be different?

Learning to get rid of the "I wants"

Another major part of the discipleship process is aligning what you want with what God wants. So, not only are you gaining Christ-centered values in the foundational stage, you are also removing self-centered desires. I like to call these your, "I wants."

If you ask most women what they want in a man, most will say a man who is tall, preferably over six feet. If you were to survey many men they would say they want a woman with a little "junk in the trunk," or they may comment on a woman's breast size. I know these wants are shallow, but it doesn't stop people from engaging or separating from someone, if they don't meet their standards.

The problem with our wants is that they might not be what God wants. That doesn't mean that all of your "I wants" are bad, but it does mean that your wants can complicate God's desire for you, particularly if you are unwilling to let them go.

Consider water, it doesn't take a lot for it to become polluted. If I offered you a fresh glass of water, how much dirt would you allow me to put in it before you refused to drink it? If I offered you food, how many times would you let me cough on it before you wouldn't eat it?

If you are seeking God for pure desires, how much self does it take to pollute those desires?

The last I checked a man's height doesn't determine his godliness, nor a woman's butt size her virtue. Yet there are numerous people who are so focused on what they want, that they don't realize they could be passing up a blessing God wants for them. "Self" will mess up a good thing if you let it.

As you grow in Christ, a transformation is taking place. The more you grow, the more you will notice a change in your relationship desires. What you used to find attractive is no longer attractive. What you thought was important, really wasn't that important. In the end you'll find you're not the same person, and that's the point of discipleship. In Christ you will become a better man. In Christ you will become a better woman. You are a new creature in Christ! Learn to give your "I wants" to God and seek what He wants for you.

Bad habits are easier to abandon today than tomorrow

WHAT ARE SOME OLD RELATIONSHIP
HABITS YOU NEED TO BREAK?

Consider your "I wants," and compare them to what God wants?

Having key accountability partners or mentors

An overlooked component of the discipleship stage is building accountability partners. These are spiritually mature Christians who are able to help you become more mature in your spiritual walk. They are able to give Biblical advice and counsel, instead of personal opinions and feelings. When it comes to life and relationship matters, avoid opinions. Avoid seeking counsel from people who will only tell you what you want to hear.

An accountability partner is more than just a leader at the church, it's someone you confide in. It's someone who knows your secrets, aspirations, weaknesses, and goals. They motivate you when you are uninspired, and help to pull you up when you are down. They kick your butt when you get off track, and challenge you to do better. Even when you try to push them away, they still love you! That's an accountability partner!

WHO IS YOUR ACCOUNTABILITY PARTNER?
list their name(s) below.

Most potential accountability partners and mentors will not walk up to you and ask to have this type of relationship. Some churches have a systematic discipleship process where you are introduced to someone who will disciple you, but they don't normally seek you out. It is important for you to seek *them* out, because you now know and understand how vital it is to your foundational relationship in Christ. If you don't have one, think now of who you can rely on to be your accountability partner?

FINAL THOUGHTS

In conclusion, the most important step you can take to finding joy in relationships is seeking to build a solid foundation in Christ! You will not only be a better person for whom you choose to marry, but you will be a better person overall. Your *Happily Ever After* doesn't necessarily begin once you get married, it can begin now, regardless of whether you ever marry. In the next stage we will talk more about finding joy and completeness apart from marriage, because marriage isn't for everyone.

Your Thoughts:

LIFE APPLICATION

◇   Take a moment and reflect on the following scriptures.

"FOR I KNOW THE PLANS I HAVE FOR YOU," DECLARES THE
LORD. "PLANS TO PROSPER YOU AND NOT TO HARM YOU,
PLANS TO GIVE YOU HOPE AND A FUTURE."
JEREMIAH 29:11, NIV

"I CAN DO ALL THINGS THROUGH CHRIST WHO
STRENGTHENS ME." PHIL. 4:13, NKJV

"WE KNOW THAT ALL THINGS WORK TOGETHER FOR GOOD
TO THOSE WHO LOVE GOD, TO THOSE WHO ARE THE CALLED
ACCORDING TO HIS PURPOSE."
ROMANS 8:28, NKJV

◇   How does believing the above scriptures provide stability in what you might be going through?

◇ In what areas are you struggling to trust God, especially in relationships?

◇ What tangible actions can you take to show trust?

WEEK ONE ASSIGNMENTS: (1) Each day this week ask God to give you strength to exemplify trust through your actions (life). When doubts creep into your mind immediately stop, pray, and refocus your thoughts. (2) Get involved in a systematic discipleship process, or a Bible teaching small group where you can grow in your faith. (3) Identify your accountability partner(s) holding you accountable in the areas mentioned in this chapter.

STAGE

2

The Framework

SATISFIED IN CHRIST

Once the foundation is complete, a house is ready for the framework, which consists of putting up wood or metal framing and attaching it to the foundation. During this process the house visually begins to take shape. I've always found this interesting, because it's not the frame that determines the shape of the house, but the foundation. The framework just happens to be what people notice.

The next important stage to your *Happily Ever After* is learning to be satisfied in Christ. Yes, even while you are single! This is where you, a follower of Christ, begin to take shape similar to a frame on a house.

> GOD WILL MEET YOU WHERE YOU ARE IN ORDER TO TAKE YOU WHERE HE WANTS YOU TO GO.
>
> ~ TONY EVANS

Take note that the framing only needs the foundation to stand. In a similar way, you only need Jesus to stand. You don't need a man or woman to make you whole. When you are rooted in Christ you don't need anyone or anything else to make you complete.

This stage helps you to understand who you are in Christ. It teaches you how to rely on God for your satisfaction and learn the disciplines necessary for building healthy platonic friendships. If you struggle to find satisfaction without a mate, what makes you think you will find satisfaction with one?

Learn who you are in Christ

One of the biggest mistakes people make is jumping into a relationship without first understanding who they are in Christ. Some Christians don't know there is a transitional phase once you give your heart to Christ.

"Therefore, if anyone is in Christ, he is a new creation; old things have passed away; behold, all things have become new" (2 Cor. 5:17).

Consider what it means to be a new creature, to be born again. When a baby comes out of their mother's womb, everything is a new experience. They really don't know what they like or dislike. They are learning who they are in an ever-changing environment. When a person gives their heart to Christ, they too are learning and changing (2Cor. 3:18). They are no longer who they were before.

It is through the discipleship process that you are transformed from a child of darkness into the image of Christ; but how does that play out in real life? What does that mean when you go out with friends? How does it apply in your marriage, or your interactions at work? Do you go to the same places? Do you act the same way? Are you willing to work the same jobs?

Understand that your likes and passions are evolving. Your do's and don'ts are being redefined. Your purpose and calling is being clarified. This is an exciting time, but it's also a vulnerable time as you wrestle with identity.

- Do you still drink alcohol?

- Should you continue listening to secular music, or watching the same movies?

- What type of men are you attracted to? You once liked the "bad boys," but is that what you still want?

- What are you looking for in a wife? Does a woman's figure play a bigger role than her character?

These questions go beyond your "likes." As you begin to understand that God has a greater purpose for your life, you should also examine your career and life goals.

- What does God want you to do?

- What are your spiritual gifts?

- Will you change jobs?

- How should you approach a troubled relationship?

These are important questions to contemplate on as you grow in Christ. Consider what would happen if you stepped into a romantic relationship during this fragile stage of your faith, without a basic understanding of your likes, passions, and calling; you might make a critical foundational mistake. Let's take Jane and John for example.

Jane was extremely excited when she went to church and gave her heart to Christ. Afterwards, she became involved in ministry. A couple of months later, she began seeing someone at church, named John. John had been a Christian much longer than Jane, and was extremely dedicated. Seeing his dedication to ministry, Jane became more active and sought to help him meet his goals. A year later they were married, and the following year they had their first child. It seemed as if Jane had everything she wanted, yet there was a void inside.

While her husband was meeting his spiritual goals, Jane didn't take much time to consider her own. As a result of John's dedication, they lived a very conservative life. For example, they never watched R rated movies, and never indulged in an occasional glass of wine. Jane loved John's dedication, but she didn't see anything Biblically wrong with watching some R rated movies or having an occasional glass of wine.

Jane faced an internal struggle. She felt the life she had come to live wasn't the life she fully wanted to live. Jane felt trapped, and never communicated these feelings to her husband. Not only did she resent her husband, but began to feel resentment towards God.

When people don't take time to learn who they are in Christ, their identity can go into flux. It may not seem critical at first, but when one rushes into a relationship, it's easy to take on the likes, passions, and callings of the person they are with. This can eventually cause a lack of fulfillment in them because they won't be living based on God's calling for them, but rather someone else's.

Do you sometimes feel insecure or lost in your relationship?

Understanding who you are in Christ will help you to be a better equipped mate. You won't feel threatened by your partner, and you'll better understand how to support them without losing yourself. You'll also be able to communicate your likes, passions, and personal callings. You will come to agreements on how your shared faith in Christ plays out in your relationship, without feeling put down or neglected. Ultimately, you'll learn how to seek satisfaction in Christ and not in someone else. We'll cover this more in the next section.

Take a couple moments and consider how God is changing you. List some of your Old likes and passions compared with your New likes and passions.

Old Likes	New Likes

"You were taught, with regard to your former way of life, to put off your old self, which is being corrupted by its deceitful desires; to be made new in the attitude of your minds; and to put on the new self, created to be like God in true righteousness and holiness" (Ephesians 4:22-24, NIV).

Learn to rely on God for your satisfaction

Satisfaction in our relationships gives us a sense of fulfillment and accomplishment. We all have desires that we want fulfilled but it can be disappointing when those desires are not met.

> If your **circumstance** never **changed, could** you be happy in Christ alone?

There are thousands of unsatisfied singles looking for a relationship to make them complete. Ironically, thousands of spouses are also unsatisfied and looking to leave their marriage to feel complete. What does this tell us? Lasting satisfaction does not come from an earthly relationship.

People will let you down, because people are not perfect. When we place our relationship on a pedestal, we set ourselves up for failure and disappointments. God will never disappoint you, because He is the same today as He is tomorrow (Heb. 13:8). As you grow in Christ, you must learn to seek your satisfaction in Christ and not in people.

If you've ever stood on something unstable and began to lose your balance, your first response might be to grab hold of an object to regain stability, but it's really a false sense of security.

How can that be?

Your footing hasn't changed, what you're standing on (your foundation) is still unstable. You only feel more secure, because you are relying on something to temporarily stabilize you.

Likewise, when people don't anchor themselves in Christ, they step into relationships on unstable ground. Rather than looking to God for stability, they look to the other person. Just as in the example above, he or she provides a sense of security and ease, but only for a moment. Soon one's life and relationship can feel like a rollercoaster. If their partner is in a good mood, life is great for a short time, but the instant the person they're with is unstable, down or angry, they become that way too, and both are miserable.

This isn't God's plan for relationships. God doesn't want you on an emotional rollercoaster. No human being or material object should have that much control over your life.

So stop giving it to them!

If you feel like your emotions are on a rollercoaster ride, (married or single) look at your foundation. Make sure you are standing

> Why are you unhappy?

on the foundation built by Christ. Give yourself a check-up from the neck up. Self-reflection is necessary to keep us from self-deception.

If you say God is your foundation, but you feel your life is on a rollercoaster, you might not be as rooted in Jesus as you thought.

There's an upside to this. Knowing better means doing better. Now that you know better you can reprioritize your energy. First, stabilize your relationship with God, then you will be in a better position to gain stability in your earthly relationships.

In Stage 1 we discussed accountability and discipleship. Communicating your dissatisfaction to a spiritual mentor is a great way of finding help so that they can walk with you through the process of regaining balance in Christ.

Another important step to seeking satisfaction in Christ is knowing your identity apart from your spouse, parents, or career. Having a meaningful relationship with Jesus will help you to understand that people and careers do not define you. Even if you're married, you need to go through the spiritual journey of understanding God's call upon your life. You also need to learn how to communicate this call and set healthy boundaries, so that your calling doesn't infringe on your spouse's call and vice-versa. This too, is where a spiritual mentor can help you through the process.

UNBREAKABLE

Relationships have their challenges, and these challenges can impact you! You can't help but feel the lows when there is tension in the home, despair when you lose your job, or betrayal when you discover you've been lied to. These circumstances can momentarily make you step out of character, but these challenges won't destroy you.

When you are rooted in Jesus, you will not be broken because of life challenges, and you definitely won't rush to divorce seeking answers.

Your joy does not come from your husband. Your satisfaction doesn't come from your wife. If they didn't give it, then they can't take it away! Too many Christians are allowing their relationships to break them because they are seeking from that relationship what it could never offer.

By putting your faith in Christ, you will be rooted and in position to be who God wants you to be in your marriage.

 ## Learn to build healthy platonic relationships

Whether single or in a relationship you should take time to build healthy platonic friendships. If you struggle here, how will you be able to build a healthy romantic relationship?

LIST SOME PEOPLE OF THE SAME SEX YOU ARE FRIENDS WITH.

List some people of the <u>opposite sex</u> you are platonic friends with.

The Bible places emphasis on the importance of friendships and the role they play in the life of a believer. Not only will some of your friends be your accountability partners, but they will help you stay rooted while waiting on marriage and help you stay focused while you are married.

Who can you call when you get lonely? What community of people are you able to laugh with and go out with? These are critical components of your life as you grow in Christ. Both same sex and opposite sex friendships play a critical role.

FRIENDSHIPS WITH THE SAME SEX

It may be hard to believe, but some struggle to build healthy friendships with people of the same sex. For whatever reason, they relate better to the opposite sex, gravitating towards them, and as a result have very few friends of the same gender. If this applies to you, don't ignore it.

Learning to build these healthy relationships should be a priority before choosing to get romantically involved with others. Not only will a lack of community support negatively impact your relationships, it also ignores God's desire for older men to teach younger men, and for older women to do the same (Titus 2:1-8).

Be intentional in building community. Don't sit back and wait for platonic friendships to find you; instead, go out and find them. Get involved in Christian men or women's groups, volunteer, or join a ministry. Put yourself in a position to meet new people at church or

at community events. Introduce yourself to members you haven't met.

If you find it difficult to connect with the same sex you may consider seeking counsel. There could be a deep-seeded issue that you are not aware of, a trauma that may affect you while dating or in marriage. I can't emphasize enough, finding the reason. The framework stage is about working on yourself, so that you are complete in Christ and ready to be that godly husband or wife for whom you would choose to marry.

> AS IRON SHARPENS IRON, SO A MAN SHARPENS THE COUNTENANCE OF HIS FRIEND.
> PROV. 27:17

FRIENDSHIPS WITH THE OPPOSITE SEX

Going from a platonic friendship to a romantic friendship is a good idea. Actually, this is one of the best ways to build a lasting marriage. However, if most of your interactions with the opposite sex turns romantic, then you may struggle with setting boundaries.

Before seeking a romantic relationship with the opposite sex, work on building a few platonic friendships. This is not a mandate, but an encouragement. There are several benefits of having friends of the opposite sex.

First, it helps you to understand that not all relationships have to be romantic. Just because you're attracted to someone doesn't mean you should become romantically involved with that person. Too often people allow attraction to be the motivating factor that moves them in and out of relationships. When in the single and satisfied stage, you are learning to be complete in Christ and not in someone else. This is for your benefit. Imagine if men and women pursued romantic relationships with anyone they found attractive! That would be ridiculous!

> Don't be so quick to change who you are in Christ for somebody else

You would be surprised by the internal struggles people have to keep their feelings of attraction in check. For the stability of your future marriage, you will want to learn this basic concept, "Though I am attracted to you, we will keep our relationship platonic."

Second, maintaining friendships with the opposite sex will help you search your feelings and keep them at bay. As you grow close to someone, your feelings towards that person may grow. While this is not a signal to move into a romantic relationship, it can be a great starting point for the future. It's important to have the discipline and understanding to know the difference. We'll talk more about some of those differences in the next chapter.

Building relationships with the opposite sex will take effort. Be intentional! Get involved in a coed, small group you can identify with like a young adult ministry, singles ministry or missions ministry. This is where your church community is critical to your

Boundaries (handwritten)

Christian development and growth.

There are valuable disciplines you will learn here that will help you in your future relationships. These disciplines are called boundaries. A person, who struggles to maintain boundaries, whether platonic or romantic, will struggle to have healthy relationships.

> *"I know what it is to be in need, and I know what it is to have plenty. I have learned the secret of being content in any and every situation, whether well fed or hungry, whether living in plenty or in want" (Phil. 4:12, NIV).*

ONCE YOU ARE MARRIED

How you interact with the opposite sex will change once you are married. It is inappropriate to maintain close interactions with friends of the opposite sex once you're married. This does not mean that you cut them off completely, but it does mean there are a new set of boundaries put in place to protect the health of your marriage.

The enemy is busy within marriages doing what he can to destroy them. He will use small issues to build resentment and division. If cutting off a relationship with an old friend will bring harmony or save your marriage, there is nothing to think about.

Your wife is your best friend and she takes precedent over any other female in your life, including your mom. Your husband is your best friend and he takes precedent over any male in your life, including your dad (Matt. 19:5).

> Are your **friendships** **negatively** or positively **impacting** **your** marriage?

This can be a controversial subject and some people passionately feel different, but it comes down to priorities. Marriage is about sacrifice. The most important person in your life after God is your spouse. It is your primary duty to make sure that nothing comes between you two. This is a valuable principle to gain a *Happily Ever After* ending.

FINAL THOUGHT

Being single is not a bad thing. Unfortunately, we live in a culture that attaches failure or incompleteness with being single, but this is a cruel lie. Not everyone is meant to marry. The apostle Paul is an example of one who dedicated his life to celibacy (1 Cor. 7:7). As you seek satisfaction in Christ, lean on God for guidance in the area of relationships. Being single offers advantages that being married does not. A person who is single has a great opportunity to be fully committed to God's calling upon their life without diversion (1 Cor. 7:32-35). This can even be seasonal. One may feel a call to singleness early in life, and then later in life feel a release to marriage. The key is to be obedient to what God has called you to.

For those who are married, this chapter applies to you as well! You don't stop seeking God's guidance for your satisfaction when you get married. You will need Him more than ever to find stability, because often you have more to manage in marriage.

If you find yourself consumed with unhappiness and dissatisfaction, you are under spiritual warfare. Your fight is not with flesh and blood! The weapons of your warfare are not carnal (2 Cor. 10:4)! The way you win the battle that seems to be consuming you is through the power of God.

Spiritual rejuvenation should be your top priority!

Your Thoughts:

LIFE APPLICATION

◇　Do you know your spiritual gifts, and how God wants to use you for His purpose?

◇　How does your distinct purpose (calling) show up in your life?

◇　Do you sometimes confuse your calling with the person you date or your spouses calling? Yes / No

◇ How can you maintain (or not lose sight of) your calling and still support your mate or spouse?

WEEK TWO ASSIGNMENT: (1) Write down the good in your life. Attach your findings on a place where you will see it and apply the scripture Philippians 4:6-9. (2) Go to spiritualgiftstest.com to learn about your spiritual gifts. (3) Each day this week journal about how you sought God for fulfillment and purpose.

The Walls:
Exterior to Interior
DATA COLLECTING FRIENDS

The exterior and interior stage of the home is the completion of the walls. You might not know it yet, but there is plenty of work that goes into completing the walls. There is electrical, plumbing, insulation, drywall, texturing and sometimes, stucco. During this stage you don't make structural changes. The framing is already set and the foundation is complete.

Your goal now is making the house move-in ready.

After you have grown in discipleship, and have learned to seek satisfaction in Christ, you are ready to look to the exterior (outside) to see who is compatible with the interior (inside). I'm referring to the process of finding that person with whom you will build your life. Some like to call this stage dating, but I prefer to call it Data Collecting Friendships (DCF).

Data Collecting Friendships

The word dating as we know it has become ambiguous. DCF is a term I've coined to refer to the process between singleness and courting to clarify any confusion. There are two elements to this term: data collecting and friendships. Let's deal with the latter first, friendships.

A critical component of this stage is understanding that you are friends. Too many people rush into a "more than friends" zone, when they like someone who mutually likes them. While you may like them, and they like you, most of the time you really do not know them just yet.

When you meet somebody, you're not really meeting them; you're meeting their representative. You're seeing what they want you to see. You're getting the best of them, because they are trying to impress you. It is only through time and building a friendship that you get to know who a person really is.

That brings us to the other word that defines this stage: Data Collecting. Interestingly enough, the word dating comes from the Latin word data.[5] When you meet a possible mate your objective should be to collect data. You want to know if you are a match. Do you share the same beliefs, do you like the same things? The only way you really know a person is to spend time around them and see how they live their life.

WHAT DOES THIS LOOK LIKE IN REAL LIFE?

I've found that some teachers share Biblical principles that sound good, but don't fully explain how a person can apply it to real life. I've narrowed down three dominant transitions that take place in the Data Collecting Friendship Stage: Eyeing, Talking and Dating. Understanding these transitions and how data collecting fits in will help you avoid major mistakes and pitfalls.

Let's start with EYEING.

Eyeing someone is just that—you're checking them out. You find something about them attractive, and have possible butterflies in your stomach when you're around them. For whatever reason, they have caught your attention. I think most people have been here, and can identify with these feelings. However, there are some things you'll want to remember while eyeing someone.

Just because you're eyeing them, does not mean that they are eyeing you. In some cases, they may have no idea you exist. Don't get caught up! Don't create some unrealistic fantasy where your feelings get hurt. You're going to find yourself attracted to people, but understand what it is, and keep your feelings in check.

YOU CAN IDENTIFY THEM BY THEIR FRUIT, THAT IS, BY THE WAY THEY ACT.
MATT. 7:16, NLT

The eyeing transition is a great time to objectively collect data. Let's be honest, once you get romantically involved with someone it's harder to see things without bias. When eyeing someone you see regularly (at church, work, gym), take note of what you see about their character. Be disciplined enough to walk away from someone you really like when you see incompatibility issues.

Finally, there are times you're eyeing someone with whom you already have a platonic friendship. Where you once did not see them as anything more than a friend has now changed. This is not a terrible thing, but be careful not to mistake someone's politeness and friendship as something more. Cleary communicate your feelings. That brings us to the next transition.

TALKING

Talking is when you desire to move past a platonic friendship and are now clearly communicating intent and interest on a deeper level. This

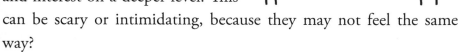

can be scary or intimidating, because they may not feel the same way?

Don't allow fear of rejection to keep you from good communication. It would be much better to know how they feel about you at the beginning, so you can properly place your feelings verses not knowing at all. Too many people miss out because they are afraid to communicate how they feel. If after communicating you need to move on, you can do so without wasting any of your time.

The talking transition may include the exchange of numbers (if you don't have them already), but it definitely includes a steady stream of communication either by phone, electronic messages or face to face communication. When both parties clearly show a common interest in each other and choose to pursue it, a romantic friendship can begin to develop that could possibly lead to courting. I believe one of the most exciting experiences within relationships is to know that someone cares for you the way you care for them.

If this is the case, try not to read more into it than you should. Continue to keep the objective in sight and your feelings in check. Remember, you need to collect data! As you talk, ask questions. Obviously, you want to temper the types of questions you ask, but your objective is to get to know them. Whenever you experience situations or events in this transition and you become uncomfortable, consider if you should move forward before you get to the third transition of the *Data Collecting Stage.*

DATING

Earlier, I mentioned that the Latin word for date was data, but the modern term for the word date is a social meeting or appointment. When a person is dating they meet regularly to enjoy one another's company whether over a meal or some other form of entertainment. Two things remain clear while dating (that is meeting regularly):

1. You are still just friends

2. You are still collecting data

This is probably the easiest transition to confuse with the next stage, courting. What makes data collecting friendships so difficult is the longer you spend time with someone you like, the more likely you are to become emotionally attached. It's easy to jump ahead and assume the relationship has evolved into something more than friendship without fully communicating that is the case.

Many people try to avoid hard discussions. Defining a relationship is one of them. Assuming you're a couple because you are close and spend time together is not the ideal way to define your relationship. As things intensify with the person you are seeing, continue to convey where you both stand in the relationship.

> Don't assume the relationship has evolved into something more than friendship without fully communicating that is the case.

Enjoy this part of the relationship without skipping the friendship stage! It's tempting to rush in and become a couple. Realize that there is nothing wrong with friends hanging out and talking with one another if you are communicating your intent. The idea that you are or must be a couple to go out on dates is silly.

Maintaining a friendship at any stage is paramount, it should start long before you get married. A solid friendship focuses on more than just passion, so don't allow sex and euphoria to guide you into a relationship.

If Married...

After you get married your friendship with your spouse should be stronger. It's unfortunate that some couples on the marriage journey have let their friendships go. That's a problem! Fluctuations in the relationship are common. Passion for each other can sometimes be up or down and the attraction for each other can also seesaw, but what should remain constant is your friendship.

I can't say this enough; your spouse is your best friend. If you find your friendship connection slipping be concerned. Start communicating so you can fix the problem in friendship. Start with the simple things. Remember the special place your spouse has in your heart. What caught your eye in the first place? Are you talking for hours the way you used to? Relive the times that bought you together.

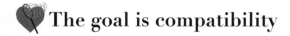 ## The goal is compatibility

Compatibility *is a state in which two things can exist or occur*
together without problems or conflict.

The reason you are collecting data is that you want to know if you're
compatible. Do you fit together? Can you work together to build a
friendship or a life together (2 Cor. 6:14)? Compatibility and
perfection are entirely different and you should know there are no
perfect men or women, but there are those who fit together
seamlessly.

Consider unleaded and diesel gases. Both are used to fuel a vehicle,
but not made for the same vehicles. If you were to put diesel fuel in
an unleaded gas engine, the car would technically work, but not for
long. Over time, the diesel fuel would hurt the regular gas engine
and eventually the car would breakdown.

This is similar in relationships. God, the designer of people and
relationships, understands that some people don't mix well. Every
person is not meant for everyone. You can
step into a relationship with someone, and
things can appear to work, but over time
critical incompatibilities will destroy the
relationship.

Every person
is not meant
for everyone.

In the *Data Collecting Stage* you first want to know, if you share the
same foundation? The scriptures clearly warn that people should not

be unequally yoked (2 Cor. 6:14). This is an agricultural analogy to say you need to share the same belief system in Christ. We already discussed in Chapter 1 why your foundation is so important. Christ shapes who you are. He defines the way you learn, grow, work, love and live. Jesus Christ impacts your very essence, because he transforms you into a new person.

> IF A MAN DOESN'T FALL ON HIS KNEES FOR PRAYER, HE DOESN'T DESERVE TO FALL TO ONE KNEE WITH A RING.
> ~ ANONYMOUS

So then, what sense would it make to build a life with someone who's foundation isn't also Christ driven? To do so would compromise the integrity of what you are building. A house cannot have two different foundations.

Though sharing the same foundation is critical, it is not the end of compatibility; it's the beginning. Many Christian's overlook the differences they have in Christ that can complicate a relationship. Yes, you heard that correctly. People can have differences in their Christian beliefs even though they share the same core faith principles in God. These differences can range from one's personal calling to a person's spiritual zeal. Let's take Frank and Staci for example.

Frank and Staci are both Christians and sincerely love God. Staci goes to church several times a week and is actively involved. Frank on the other hand goes to church once, maybe twice a month. He's not really active in ministry, nor has a desire to become active. Frank and Staci met at church and at first glance they seemed to be compatible. After a brief courtship they got engaged and married. But within the first couple months they experienced challenges around their passions.

Staci became frustrated because she felt rushed to leave church, and pressured not to participate throughout the week. Frank felt frustrated, because Staci wanted him to be actively involved in church like she is. These frustrations might not seem like a big deal, but they really are. Overtime, it can strain the marriage and if it goes unresolved, bitterness toward one another can set in.

When data collecting, be sure to ask key questions so that you can avoid spiritual challenges that may render you incompatible and hurt you later in marriage. Don't allow attraction to blind you. Here are examples of key questions you should know.

1. Do they read their Bible?
2. Are they active in church?

3. How do they incorporate Christian principals in their daily life?

4. Do they curse or drink?

5. Do they pray?

6. Do they ever offer to pray with you?

7. How do they feel about you serving in ministry?

8. Do they listen to secular music?

These are a few spiritual questions that can vary from Christian to Christian and should be considered when data collecting.

In Chapter 2 we highlighted what you value. Not all the items you value are spiritual and fall under the command of being equally yoked, but they do play a role in compatibility. For instance, some people value tidiness more than others. Some people are loud and boisterous while others are quiet and reserved. Some people are sticklers about money and budgeting and some live extremely carefree. You have socializers versus those who enjoy solitary and some people desire a big family when others, not so much.

None of these make you a horrible person, but they can have a big impact on your relationships. Let's say you're big on eating healthy and working out. If you date someone who has no desire to eat healthy or make efforts to work out, you need to pause and consider what your marriage will look like in the future. Are you prepared to live with that reality for the rest of your life?

What about aspirations and goals? Let's say someone has aspirations to be a nurse. Are you prepared to support your spouse working long and sometimes sporadic hours? If their intended desires is to do mission work, would you be willing to live in a third world country or have them away for weeks at a time? Have you truly considered how their occupation or ministry will impact your marriage, or how your dreams will impact them?

In relationships you make compromises, but you need to decide which of those compromises you can live with for the rest of your life, and which ones you can't, data collecting.

I've come to believe and share a question that all couples considering marriage should ask. If your fiancée never changed, could you love them for the rest of your life just the way they are? This is not to say someone can't change or that you can't pray for change. This question merely helps you to understand that when you marry someone, you are marrying what you see, not what you hope to get. Otherwise, if a person doesn't change, you might find yourself unwilling to sacrifice and love them unconditionally.

> If your **fiancée**
> **never** changed,
> could you **love**
> **them** for **the rest**
> of **your life** just
> the way **they are?**

Remaining friends during the *Data Collecting Stage* keeps you from getting attached too quickly. It gives you time to learn more about the person you are interested in. If you see major concerns, you can remain in the friendship stage or you can share that you don't see the relationship continuing. Breaking-up is not easy, but it is easier to break-up when you are not allowing emotions to control your decision-making.

If Married... When you are married the goal is to stay married and compatible. It's easy to grow apart over time if you allow it to happen. Before you know it, work, kids, hobbies and church can take up most of your time. You can look up and it's been months, even years, since you and your spouse have been on a date. Don't let that happen.

Keep dating and romancing your spouse to maintain compatibility. Some married couples find it hard to have a date night. It is your obligation to keep dating for the health of your relationship. Keep it simple and learn to be friends again if you have drifted away. Have fun with each other. Your moments together should be fun and interesting and leave the serious business-focused conversations at the office.

Work on good communication

There has been a reoccurring theme throughout this stage. Communication. I wanted to give communication its own section, because people are so darn awful at it.

Although, it can be hard at times to communicate how you feel, it is the difference between a *Happily Ever After*, and a Happily Ever NOT! It's why the guy gets the girl and the girl gets the guy. It's why people don't get too invested in dead-end relationships, and it's why a good friendship can turn into a great marriage. Therefore don't start working on good communication when you get married. Build good communication habits in the friendship stage.

TO BE SLOW TO ANGER MEANS YOU ARE WILLING TO WORK WITH WRONG OVER TIME.

~ DAVID POWLISON

When you are data collecting it is important to continually discuss where the friendship is headed. Romantic friendships should evolve. How long this process will last depends on the couple. For some, this stage can last one to two months; for others, it can last up to a year. In the end, communication is the key.

Good communication is something you learn and is something you have to work towards. You don't come out of your mother's womb with good communication skills. If you find yourself struggling to talk about important issues when single and dating, what makes you think you'll talk about them when courting and married?

Read books on good communication, such as *Good and Angry,* by David Powlison, or *Now You're Speaking My Language,* by Gray Chapman. Learn to be quick to hear and slow to speak (James 1:19). Don't think about your response while someone is talking, and in some circumstances repeat back what they are trying to communicate to ensure understanding.

Finally, whatever you do, try not to use electronic messaging to communicate important matters. Electronic messaging is easy and convenient, but is horrible at communicating tone. A reader can easily misinterpret the message as hostile. If there is an intense topic that needs to be discussed, wait till you can call or talk in person.

Guard your heart in this stage

I've mentioned this a couple times thus far, but now I want to go into detail. Don't allow your infatuation to blind you to critical information. Don't allow your impatience to move you forward into something too quickly. If you can learn to temper your feelings you will avoid mistakes in the *Data Collecting Stage* and this is how you do it.

First, understand what you are feeling. Is what I'm feeling euphoric, hormonal, or love? All have their value and place in a relationship, but they are not the same. Just because you really like someone, doesn't mean you are prepared to love them.

You will find yourself extremely excited (euphoric) to find someone who likes you just as much as you like them. The more you spend time together the more your feelings will grow towards them. That's okay, but where this can turn destructive is when your feelings take control of your decision making. The scriptures warn us several times not to trust in our feelings (Proverbs 3:5-6).

Couples who are unable to control their feelings are those who have sex before marriage, when they vowed not to. They are couples who marry too quickly (with no foundation, framework, or data) and later regret their decision. They are also those in dead-end relationships, going nowhere, but unable to break it off because of emotional attachments.

Since, love never fails; LOVE is greater than a feeling. Love does what euphoria won't. Love pushes past where sexual stimulation stops. Love is not a word that you say, but the action that you take.

> YOUR HEART IS PRECIOUS TO GOD SO
> GUARD IT AND WAIT FOR THE PERSON
> WHO WILL TREASURE IT
> ~ ANONYMOUS

PHYSICAL DISPLAYS OF AFFECTION

What would you consider appropriate forms of physical affection while in the friendship stage?

The second way you guard your heart is... Don't underestimate the power of physical displays of affections. Physical touch goes a long away. There are moments that just a rub of a person's shoulder can stimulate you. It's what makes holding hands, kissing, and affectionate rubs so pleasurable. Don't fool yourself! Often these are forms of foreplay especially when you haven't had sex with them yet. Though kissing and holding hands is not sinful; it does impact your feelings, and communicates that the relationship is something more than friendship.

> Don't fool yourself; often these are forms of foreplay especially for those who haven't had sex together.

Many people have grown up watching movies or hearing of the guy who kisses the girl at the end of the first date. It's supposed to be romantic, but is it wise? In many cases, you are strangers with a person on a first date. You are not a couple. You might not even be friends, so why are you kissing?

What I'm saying might be challenging for some of you reading this, and may sound too conservative, but please bear with me.

If I were to ask you what forms of physical touch are appropriate between friends, most of you would stop at holding hands. A kiss says something! A touch says something more. These are indicators that you are more than friends.

These forms of connection also cause you to become emotionally attached whether you know it or not.

The goal to guarding your heart is to maintain healthy boundaries. A relationship that lacks healthy boundaries is a relationship doomed to fail. This is why the first two stages are so important. Both your foundation in Christ and satisfaction in Christ, help build your boundaries. Your why in what you do!

> A relationship that lacks healthy boundaries is a relationship doomed to fail.

Sex is something special that was created by God for marriage. Therefore, you should set boundaries to prevent yourself from engaging in sex before marriage. You show me someone who had consensual sex before marriage and I will show you someone who struggled to maintain boundaries.

If you want to find success and avoid pitfalls while searching for a spouse, then guard your heart. A person needs to earn something as precious as your emotions. As someone shows themselves trustworthy of your heart, you can slowly give them a place in it.

If Married... After you get married you want to be mindful of how your emotions and feelings impact your decision making. In this section I pointed out how dating couples can rush into a relationship, because of positive feelings; the same is true for couples rushing out of a marriage because of negative feelings.

Control your feelings as you find yourself becoming emotionally detached from your spouse! Many marriages will experience emotional highs and lows. When you find your feelings on a low trend, be careful that you do not let those feelings control your decision making. These can be feelings of anger, betrayal, displeasure, unhappiness, or disgust. The enemy will use these feelings to move you off your foundation. Hold on to Christ. Hold on to your values and continue to trust in God.

Remember what love is. Love never fails! Love hopes, when you feel despair. Love believes, when you feel lost. Love endures, when feelings fade.

Ask God to give you strength to love and to deal with your anger and frustrations in constructive ways.

Maintain community involvement

Community is an important part in every stage of the relationship process. In the foundational stage, accountability partners came from your community. In the framework, they were your platonic friendships. In the Data Collecting Stage, they are the ones who help you stay level headed and maintain boundaries.

Too many couples isolate themselves early in the relationship process, and by the time they resurface, they are already emotionally attached and or have possibly negotiated key boundaries. Therefore, maintaining community is for your protection and support, allowing a healthy relationship to blossom.

I don't think most people intentionally detach from their community but doing so can be effortless. While single, it's no surprise that much of your social interaction is with your community. When you meet someone there is often a natural pull to spend time with that person. Unfortunately, this can come at a cost, and that cost is your support. This is where you have to be intentional.

Group dating is a great way to keep your community involved in the *Data Collecting Stage*. This doesn't have to be your conventional couple paring. This can involve singles as well. Maybe there is a ministry fellowship, or a group of friends going out. Organize a fun night with friends and invite your person of interest. The key is to keep your community involved early in the process verses later.

SEEING WHAT YOU DON'T

The longer you build a romantic friendship the harder it is for you to see things objectively. Let's call it googly-eyed. This is normal, but it can be harmful when you overlook critical red flags. Having that friend who can see things objectively, may see what you do not see. They encourage you when you feel tempted to let go of your boundaries, and correct you when you've crossed a line.

Listen to their advice. Communicate with them throughout the process. These should be key people whom you trust and hold you to the boundaries you set. Your community can be your accountability partners, mentors, pastors, ministry leaders, and church family. Take a moment and write down who is actively involved in your data collecting process who is spiritually mature and offering spiritual guidance?

> BEING IN LOVE IN THE BEGINNING OF A RELATIONSHIP IS LIKE AN ILLNESS. IT IS TREATABLE, BUT IT IS AN ILLNESS NEVERTHELESS. THE ILLNESS IS THE INABILITY TO SEE REALITY.
>
> ~ HENRY CLOUD

If
Married... Isolation isn't a good thing while dating, nor is it good while married. Don't withdraw from your community, especially during tough times. Staying connected may take more effort, but it is well worth it to keep your marriage strong.

The easiest way to maintain community-connection while married is getting involved in a couples' ministry. There are two things you should look for in a couples' ministry. First, if they meet regularly and discuss relationship problems and solutions? Second, do they have occasional group date nights that you can participate in?

Don't limit your couple groups to *your* church, and know that if your church doesn't provide what you need, explore what your local community has to offer. This doesn't mean you have to leave your church and join another. It might even be a good idea to start a couples ministry. You don't have to have the perfect marriage or know everything to lead a couples group. All you need is a willing heart, an open home and Biblical principles.

FINAL THOUGHTS

There is a lot that happens in the *Data Collecting Stage*, and it can happen fast. If this is your current phase of life, I encourage you to reread this chapter. Evaluate how you are implementing the key principles shared. Who are your accountability partners involved in your life while you date? Are you actively communicating with them and listening to their advice?

There are also many important events that happen in this stage to build friendships and romance. If you are married, pay close attention to the notes at the end of each section highlighting how the chapter applies to you. Continue to cultivate your friendship with your spouse.

Finally, maintain an active prayer life. Intentional prayer while dating will keep God in the forefront of your process. Asking Him for wisdom and guidance is critical to avoiding relationship landmines. Don't lean on your own understanding, but listen and trust God and He will guide you through the relationship process (Prov. 3:5-6).

Your Thoughts

LIFE APPLICATION

◇   What are non-negotiable's for you when seeking
    compatibility with someone?

◇   On a scale from one to ten, how well do you communicate
    your feelings? (___) Learn better communication skills
    by journaling your feelings and looking for ways to better
    communicate them.

◇   What forms of physical touch do you struggle with? Have
    you told your accountability partners?

◇ How are you intentionally keeping your community involved with those you are dating/interested in?

◇ How are you intentionally keeping your community involved in your marriage?

WEEK THREE ASSIGNMENT:

Unmarried: (1) Schedule a date with your pastor or spiritual mentor to meet the person you are building a romantic bond with. (2) Write down specific boundaries you plan to maintain when it comes to physical affection, both in the friendship and courtship stages.

Married: (1) Take your spouse on a date this week, and make it special. (2) Don't over complicate your marriage. Be your spouse's best friend and enjoy each other.

4

The Details

COURTING WITH INTENT

The fourth stage of building a house is all about the details. This is the stage where the owner gives the house its personal touch: flooring, wall color, faucets, lighting fixtures, kitchen accessories, and more. The house is nearly complete and almost ready to be occupied.

In a similar way, the fourth stage of a relationship is all about the final details that cement the relationship before marriage. I call this stage courting with intent. When you are courting, there is a clear end goal. Using the label *courting* gives everyone involved the understanding of the purpose. Out of all the stages this one is probably the easiest.

Courting makes the relationship official

In this stage, there should be no confusion about where your relationship stands and where you are headed. You have moved from the friendship stage to a couple who is *seriously* considering marriage. You are exclusive, and not looking elsewhere.

Some people struggle with commitment. Maybe they've been hurt, or they simply aren't ready to settle down. Intentional or not, don't allow someone to tie you down to an exclusive relationship without being committed to its end goal.

> Don't allow someone to tie you down to an exclusive relationship without being committed to its end goal.

Those who want to avoid commitment find crafty and unique ways to do so. One of the ways people avoid commitment is to simply not talk about it. This doesn't necessarily shed a negative light on them, everyone has his or her challenges. If you find that your relationship is stalling, you should address it. Don't allow fear of the relationship ending keep you from communicating. Avoidance of the conversation from either side is a sign that you didn't communicate well in stage three and did not maintain healthy boundaries. If you had, having this type of discussion would be easier.

Ultimately, relationships are meant to progress. A relationship shouldn't stay in the Data Collecting nor the Courting stage indefinitely. There are different thoughts on how long it should take before a couple gets married. Some people say less than a year is not long enough, others will say more than four years is too long. The Bible really doesn't give a number, but I believe there are dangers in both, so allow me to offer my godly advice and you can pray on the subject.

How are you avoiding a dead end relationship?

Though there are those who have beaten the odds by getting married (and staying married) after dating and courting for less than a year; they are a rare exception. Studies have shown that people who rush into marriage, unfortunately also rush into divorce[6]. Extending your courtship will lead to better odds of staying married. On the other hand, courting for an extended time can lead to a dead-end relationship, especially if your courtship last longer than four years with no marriage date in sight.

Being in a dead-end relationship can be frustrating, and it would be natural to feel stuck. If you have invested years into the relationship, walking away won't be easy and at this point it could go on for another four to five years with the same results. Trust God with your future, and don't let fear keep you from communicating.

HOW LONG SHOULD YOU WAIT TO GET MARRIED?

I believe a one to three-year courtship is average and a good place to be. Every situation is different, but a good rule of thumb is this: if you have a short friendship stage, increase your courtship stage. If you have a long friendship stage, then there's nothing wrong with a shorter courtship.

There are some couples who have been friends for years, and later became romantically involved. They have collected the data and know each other well. On the other hand, some couples step into a romantic relationship only knowing each other for a short while. In this scenario it will take time for them to really learn what they need to know about each other. If this is you, go back and reread Stage 3, Compatibility. In the end, let the Holy Spirit and godly counsel guide you through this time.

Courting forms greater bonds

One of the things that makes courting serious is that your lives begin to fuse. Though you are not one in marriage yet, you do begin to share a life. You dream together, set goals, and aspire for the best, because you are building together.

At this point, it's okay to begin to let your guard down and allow yourself to become more emotionally attached. By this time, you should have received enough data where you can trust that person with your heart. This isn't a decision solely based on feelings. They have invested and shown themselves to be committed to you and a future together.

As time passes and you grow closer, you'll also find your pronouns begin to change. No longer will you speak in the singular, but in the plural (we, our, us). This shouldn't be a forced action, but rather natural as the goal is a life together.

Fusing is a natural progression. When making big decisions from vacations to the purchase of a vehicle, realize your plans may impact the person you are courting, and vice-versa. Therefore, you should want their opinion. While you don't need their approval, it's wise to include them in the process, because your debt could ultimately become theirs should you wed.

If you find yourself struggling to fuse, or you find that your partner is struggling with this, take note! This is a great opportunity for... you guessed it, communication. Ask why they might be struggling to include you in their plans? Ask yourself, "Why is it hard for me to let them into areas of my life?"

Theses are the details you want to pay attention to. They are also opportunities for personal growth. People are constantly learning and growing in relationships. Just because a person struggles with commitment, doesn't mean you should dump them. Some people don't realize they have commitment issues until they go through the process.

Ultimately, don't ignore the issues. There are couples that have been together for years and still haven't met each other's immediate family. Why the distance and hesitation? It shouldn't take over a year to meet close relatives, especially if they live in the same area. If there's a problem with their family accepting you or your family accepting them, then these are things you need to discuss. This won't just go away. It's going to impact your marriage, your children, and holidays. Are you prepared for that type of dysfunction?

Final note: If there appears to be any form of secrecy, do not accept or excuse it. There should not be secrets between a husband and wife.

DO NOT PASS GO! Do Not Collect $200

If the idea of marriage and exclusivity is too much for you and feel you are not ready for commitment, you should not be pursuing a relationship beyond friendship. Otherwise, it  is selfish to pull on someone's heart and get into a committed relationship when you know marriage is not in your future. Communicate your intent and remain friends.

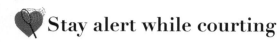 Stay alert while courting

During the *Courting Stage* be observant and alert! Though you have gained enough positive information to move into this stage, you don't want to ignore possible problems such as those mentioned in this chapter.

Pay attention to how your partner responds to life's challenges. Take notice of how they act when they're tired. How they handle struggles with money, work issues, or their attitude when they don't get their way. You should look for them to compromise and work on a solution. When you have a disagreement do they shut down and shut you out? Do you shut down and shut them out? These are not healthy forms of communication. Be aware that relationship struggles don't magically improve during marriage.

Some of these problems are deal-breakers, and some of them are not. Ultimately, what you want to know the most is if he or she is open to growth. For example, if someone struggles with poor communication or bad temperament and is unwilling to acknowledge their shortcomings, you should be concerned.

The courting stage is also a great time to ask deeper questions. These can be complex questions that you wouldn't ask during the friendship stage such as what was your childhood like? Was your father a part of your life? Did you suffer childhood trauma (abuse or abandonment)? Why aren't you close to your mom? Have you ever had a communicable disease?

Be prayerful on how to approach these topics. They are not easy discussions, and you will most likely feel uncomfortable having them, but they are extremely important! When planning a life together someone's past will ultimately have an impact on your future. Knowing about and understanding their history will help you both be better partners to each other.

If you experience major relationship problems, don't be afraid to slow things down. Everyone has a past, so it doesn't mean it has to end the relationship, but it should be contemplated. Marriage is for life. Taking a step back or slowing things down to address problematic areas is wise, especially when considering you're going to spend the rest of your life together. You would much rather gain clarity on issues before marriage, than be blindsided by them after marriage.

WHAT WOULD WORRY YOU THE MOST IF YOU WERE TO CALL OFF AN ENGAGEMENT?

"Worrying won't stop the bad stuff from happening; It just stops you from enjoying the good."

Don't let fear rule this stage of the relationship.

Finally! Don't rush to move in

Too many Christians go from friends, to courting, to marriage, too fast! As I mentioned earlier don't stall, but don't rush either! It's tempting to rush when you find somebody you like and the feelings are mutual. I believe this is a greater temptation among people who choose to wait to have sex until marriage. As they desire to hold to God's standard, the couple fights the urge to be intimate. The excitement and urge for intimacy often causes a celibate couple to move quicker through the relationship process into an early marriage.

Remember, if what you are building is for life, then there's no rush. Seriously, if he or she is threatening to leave the relationship because you want a longer courtship, you have a bigger problem than the length of your courtship.

Allow the relationship to progress, but convenience and horniness should not be in the equation. Building something solid takes time. Keep your community involved and allow them to help you stay encouraged when you become frustrated and impatient.

Set goals for the relationship. This will help you keep your eye on the prize and feel satisfied that the relationship is progressing. If you do decide to get engaged within a year, then set the marriage date a year to a year and a half from the engagement. You will be surprised how fast the time goes.

Set boundaries to avoid premarital sex. By this time, couples are displaying some forms of physical intimacy such as: kissing, holding hands, and affectionate rubs. Though these can be innocent, they can also be a form of foreplay that is too tempting. The urge to have sex before marriage can be extremely strong. Communicate your boundaries, and have a plan in place. Avoid situations that may leave you vulnerable in the moment. There are plenty of people who thought they were in control, only to find themselves out of control.

Lastly, take time to get pre-marital counseling. The point of this counseling isn't designed to talk you out of marriage, but rather, to give you the tools necessary for a long-lasting marriage. Don't rush through the process!

FINAL THOUGHTS

Finding a life-long husband or wife is a wonderful experience. Soak in this time you are sharing, and try not to lose it once you get married. Enjoy one another, but continue to stay alert. During this phase the enemy will use temptations to spoil the unique gift of offering each other sexual purity on your wedding night. Don't let that happen! Don't let one moment ruin years of celibacy.

Finally, be on alert for major red flags. At this point you have invested a lot of time and energy, making it more difficult to take a step back, or break it off altogether, but turning a blind eye isn't the answer. Don't view marriage as the fix-all to problems; in reality it only adds new challenges. If you have major reservations about certain areas, seek counsel! In some situations, it may be better to talk with the counselor privately to gain clarity of thought and direction. The Bible tells us, "Where there is no counsel, the people fall; but in the multitude of counselors there is safety (Proverbs 11:14)."

Your Thoughts

LIFE APPLICATION

◇   Do you struggle to make relationships official, or are you
     with someone who struggles? Why do you think that is?

◇   Do you sometimes find yourself being anxious and
     wanting to rush the relationship? Yes or No, WHY?

◇ Do you sometimes find yourself being anxious and rushing to end your marriage? Yes or No, WHY?

◇ When was the last time you had marriage counseling?

WEEK FOUR ASSIGNMENT:

Unmarried: (1) Pray and ask God to take away any anxieties you may have, and to reveal his desires for you. (2) Build on good communication and ask the deeper questions. (3) Talk with the person you are seeing and clarify where you are in the relationship process, and where it's headed. (4) Make a plan and set a date to start pre-marital counseling.

Married: (1) Pray and ask God to take away any anxieties you may have, and to reveal his desires for you. (2) Schedule a marriage counseling session regardless of whether or not you feel you need it. (3) Don't overlook the small things in your marriage. Take time this week to observe and listen. Journal a list of things that your spouse cares about.

5

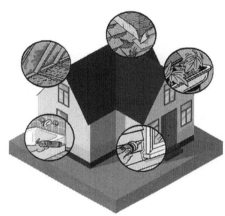

The Maintenance

When you finish building a house the work hasn't ended; in actuality, it has just begun. You are committing to a lifetime of labor and maintaining the home. A house that is not maintained will fall apart over time; destroying the effort it took to build it in the first place.

The focus within the last stage of the relationship process is making sure your marriage stays healthy! Don't view getting married as the finish line, but rather the starting line. It is the beginning of a

> Don't **view** **getting** married as the **finish** line, but rather the **starting** line.

beautiful life-long commitment. The finish line is staying married.

The idea of looking at marriage as maintenance is not too appealing because maintenance is work! No one gets excited to do chores? But, if you don't clean, you get bugs. If you don't wash your clothes, you run out of things to wear. You get where I am going. You can't have the benefits of a good marriage without putting in the work.

Those who can grasp this part of marriage will be in the right mindset to have a *Happily Ever After* ending. On the other hand, those who struggle to understand their responsibility to cultivate their marriage will find it challenging at every turn.

♥ Marriage requires sacrifice

I hate to be the bearer of bad news, but... you're selfish! Don't take it personally; we're all selfish, and for the most part we enter relationships with selfish motives.

Let's be honest, during the dating phase, if the experience isn't positive for the most part, you are not going to marry that person. You will conclude that it's not meant to be and most likely move on. Yet in marriage, there is a shift, marriage requires you to be selfless.

Love, by definition, is sacrificial. Jesus said in John 15:12, "This is My commandment, that you love one another as I have loved you." Those who struggle to sacrifice will struggle in marriage. Those who find success in marriage are those who *learn* to be givers, helpers, and one who sacrifices. Note that I said, "learn." Some people have a natural gift of giving, but for others, this is not the case, it's something they learn to do every day.

Though relationships are give and take, your giving is not contingent upon you getting. I cannot tell you how many couples struggle with this concept. People don't mind giving as long as they're getting, but there are times in a marriage when your needs are not going to be met. This is not the time to retreat from your responsibilities. This is what it means to sacrifice. It's not a sacrifice if it doesn't cost you anything. Jesus loves you even though your gifts will never measure up to His.

There are many scriptural examples that talk about the sacrifice of relationships, but one I would like to highlight is found in 1 Corinthians 7 and directly addresses the husband and wife.

> *"The husband should fulfill his marital duty to his wife, and likewise the wife to her husband" (1 Cor. 7:3, NIV).*

The husband is to meet the needs of his wife and the wife the needs of her husband. Imagine for a moment, if a couple actually did this. Rather than the husband looking to meet his needs, he seeks to meet his wife's needs instead. Imagine the wife doing the same.

Something amazing would happen! Their individual needs would both be met. Mind blowing, isn't it?

In the end, if loving sacrificially were easy it wouldn't be a sacrifice. Loving your spouse sacrificially takes power that you don't have. This is where your foundation comes in. It's your connection to God that gives you the power to love the way Jesus loves.

Learn to trust God in difficult moments and not rely on your feelings. Your feelings can lead you astray and cause you to quit.

SACRIFICING FOR YOUR SPOUSE doesn't mean you are a doormat; it means that you are willing to put pride aside and ask What Would Jesus Do, WWJD?

- How would Jesus respond?

- How would Jesus love?

- How would Jesus help?

Don't focus on what your spouse is or isn't doing. Examine whether you are part of the problem or the solution. Let God deal with your spouse; you just obey and trust Him.

There are no lease to buy options

A lease is when a person receives full benefits without committing to buy. In the case of a house, they live in it, sleep in it, bathe in it, entertain in it and more, but at any time they can walk away from it without the commitment. When people allow someone to experience sexual benefits from them or live with them without being married, they are allowing themselves to be leased with an option to buy (marriage). I know this can sound harsh, but that's the point.

Don't cheapen yourself or the relationship. These are sacred experiences only meant for a married couple. You ought to think more highly of yourself! Even if you are not a virgin, God says you are a new creature in Him. Start now by reserving sex and other marital experiences for when that time comes. When you do tie the knot, your marriage will have that much more value.

> IF ALL HE WANTS IS BREAST, LEGS, AND THIGHS SEND HIM TO KFC.
> ~ ANONYMOUS

Consider William, he had his mind made up that he would abstain from sex until marriage and communicated this to his girlfriend, Olivia. She seemed excited that he held these Christian values, so they chose not to touch while watching a movie to keep temptations at bay.

Whenever they were alone she pushed the limits. Soon after, their resolve waned. The couple began to cuddle, which led to kissing. William tried to stop things from escalating, but time and time again Olivia pushed the boundaries. Before long, William and Olivia gave in to sex, breaking their commitment. The saddest part is neither of them fully enjoyed the experience because they were overwhelmed with guilt afterwards.

A lack of boundaries resulted in an abuse of privileges. Note that Olivia took advantage by not keeping her commitment to God and to William. However, William did not use good judgment when Olivia pushed the issue; he should have stayed true to his beliefs and to his commitment to God as well.

If someone truly loves you, they will not seek to take advantage of you. They will be willing to make sacrifices for you, because they value you and your principles.

"You say, "Food for the stomach and the stomach for food, and God will destroy them both." The body, however, is not meant for sexual immorality but for the Lord, and the Lord for the body" (1 Corinthians 6:13, NIV).

The family makes the home

When people get married they're excited to finally live what they have dreamt about for so long. Yet, reality doesn't always match the fantasy. I've seen couples have what appeared to be the picture-perfect marriage, yet, they're not happy!

How does this happen? The reason is simple, a happy marriage consists of more than the "things" in it. Priorities can get misplaced. The couple begins to focus on their children and their sports, the school, the home, their jobs, church, activities, and various situations surrounding these areas of life. Before long, these circumstances take priority over their marriage.

> A happy marriage consists of more than the "things" in it.

There's an old saying that speaks to this point; a house does not make a home.

When Andre and Shay first got married they lived in a one-bedroom apartment. They didn't have much, but they didn't struggle and were happy. After having their first child they became increasingly discontented with their living situation.

They considered moving into a two-bedroom apartment, however they crunched the numbers and decided that if Andre worked extra hours, and if they cut back on extra-curricular activities, they could instead afford a four-bedroom house. At first Andre and Shay were excited! They were homeowners, living the dream! Yet that excitement soon turned into frustration.

Unfortunately, they only had one car, and Andre needed it for work. As a result, Shay felt trapped being stuck at home. When the child got old enough for daycare, they decided Shay would start working full-time. This way they could purchase another car and have some spare cash. Fast-forward two years. From the outside Andre and Shay appear to have a happy marriage. They have a beautiful family, active in church, a nice home and two new cars, but on the inside their marriage is falling apart.

Andre and Shay hadn't been on a date in over a year. Most of their time together was spent arguing about money or their child's activities. Shay felt neglected, because Andre was rarely home, and she shouldered most of the responsibility of raising their child. Andre felt frustrated, because he was often at work, and when he did arrive home, Shay appeared to always be upset. Bitterness and anger over time will tear this couple apart, all because they lost sight of the most important thing after God.

EACH OTHER!

Your spouse is your top priority. The family is more important than your house, job, money, schooling, parents, in-laws, and friends. You should not be trying to keep up with the Joneses. You should be meeting the needs of your spouse and maintaining a healthy marriage. If you and your spouse are good, than everything else will fall in place. But if you are putting your career and other non-essentials before your spouse, your life is out of order. No one should come before your partner in marriage.

I'm not suggesting that you neglect the goals you may want to pursue, what I am saying is that you don't neglect your marriage while you pursue those goals.

For example, when a husband has his life ordered properly, he may be willing to turn down a promotion at work if it causes conflict at home. He would discuss the options with his wife... communication. If she understands his aspirations and pushes him to take the promotion, he pursues it, because he communicated with her, making sure her needs would still be met. If for some reason, after taking the job her needs were no longer being met, he would prayerfully consider a demotion to prevent division in their marriage.

> THE KEY ISN'T TO PRIORITIZE WHAT'S ON YOUR SCHEDULE, BUT TO SCHEDULE YOUR PRIORITIES
>
> ~ STEPHEN COVEY

These are things to contemplate and should always be in the forefront of a marriage. Many marriages are destroyed, because couples neglect each other trying to *live the dream*. A big house is great and climbing the career ladder is awesome, but if you lose sight of your union the dream will crumble. The best gift you can ever give your spouse is a healthy marriage, not stuff!

Don't overcomplicate your marriage. Keep it simple by maintaining your priorities. God is always first and the foundation of your life. Your spouse is second. The scriptures clearly highlight the precedence a spouse takes in one's life (Eph. 5:25). Your children come next and after that comes your purpose or calling. All of the other pulls on your life come last. They might include your occupation, school, extended family, and so on, and not in any specific order.

Marriage is for life

"So then, they are no longer two but one flesh.
Therefore what God has joined together,
let not man separate" (Matt. 19:6).

I don't believe the average person steps into marriage thinking divorce. Most people have a deep conviction that their marriage will last. Yet for many, somewhere along the journey their view changes. What was never a thought can eventually permeate the brain. So, what happened?

Adversity happened!

There are few things more disturbing and frightening than feeling that you are in a doomed marriage. Where can you go when you wake up everyday feeling trapped and lonely? How do you fix a broken heart? It is in these moments that hopelessness can set in. When a person loses hope they begin to lose sight of God, because God is the author of hope.

WIN THE BATTLE OF THE MIND

A major part of obtaining your *Happily Ever After* ending is winning the battle of your mind. You don't just wake up one day and speak the word divorce. No! That thought is in a person's mind long before they speak it. It's a thought they have allowed to turn over in their mind so many times that it has begun to overshadow a greater truth! God is able!

> If God can resurrect the dead, surely He can resurrect a marriage.

If God can resurrect the dead, surely, He can resurrect a marriage, but you must believe it. When you allow divorce to become an option it changes your possibilities. It offers an escape route that leads to nowhere!

Consider what it takes to raise a child. Children will drive you crazy at times. Being a parent has its challenges; some of those challenges are greater than others and some are down-right depressing. Feelings of hopelessness can begin to set in for any parent, but during those challenges, a parent would not consider divorcing their twelve-year-old child. It's not an option, instead, they would seek to restore the relationship and help the child.

This should be no different in marriage. If divorce is not an option, your mindset should be seeking solutions. Ultimately, working on solving your issues keeps you engaged in the marriage verses being detached.

GOD HATES DIVORCE

God's position on divorce hasn't changed. He hates it (Malachi 2:16). God knows the destruction divorce brings on the family and the community. Your position should be God's position, because God is your foundation.

If you find yourself disengaging from your marriage, ask God to help you with your thinking. Don't allow the enemy to put negative thoughts in your head where they can consume you. One of my favorite scriptures comes from Phil 4:8-9.

"Finally, brethren, whatever things are true, whatever things are noble, whatever things are just, whatever things are pure, whatever things are lovely, whatever things are of good report, if there is any virtue and if there is anything praiseworthy— meditate on these things. The things which you learned and received and heard and saw in me, these do, and the God of peace will be with you" (Phil. 4:8-9).

It's hard "not" to have negative thoughts pass through your mind, but you have the control and you can prevent negative thoughts from becoming your meditation. Note that what you think about is directly linked to your peace. When you are able to follow Philippians 4:8-9 God promises that His peace will be with you.

> What you think about is directly linked to your peace.

For every negative, God gives us a positive. We just have to see it. I've learned in my journey that gratitude is willful perspective. It's what you choose to focus on. For example, two people become paralyzed after a tragic car accident. One falls into depression, because he only focuses on what he can't do and the way things used to be. The other survivor lives a vibrant and happy life because he focuses on what he can do, and life's possibilities. Both individuals faced the same challenge, but their viewpoints resulted in different outcomes.

Ask God to help you see what He sees, to hear what He hears, to go where He tells you to go, and to love how He loves! Win the daily battle of your mind.

IMPORTANT NOTE:

Please don't misunderstand what I am saying in this section. When I say not to focus on divorce, I'm not telling someone to stay in an abusive relationship. If a spouse is experiencing any form of abuse, they need to remove themselves from that dangerous situation immediately and seek outside help.

With spiritual help and guidance, they can gain safety, healing and clarity on how to move forward. Remember that even in these challenges, God is still at work. He is not the cause of such evils, but He is the solution, offering hope to those who are drowning in hopelessness. Winning the battle of your mind is even more critical in the midst of facing evil. Always remember: "Greater is He that is in us than he who is in the world (1John 4:4)."

A NEGATIVE MIND WILL NEVER
GIVE YOU A POSITIVE LIFE.

~ ZIAD ABDELNOUR

Your Thoughts

LIFE APPLICATION

◇   Do you desire to get married? Are your actions reflective of a giver, helper or one who sacrifices?

◇   Are the actions of the person you intend to marry reflective of a giver, helper or one who sacrifices?

◇   In what ways do you show that your marriage is a priority?

◇ Love goes above and beyond; it sacrifices for the other. What sacrifices do you need to make that "your spouse" cares about?

◇ It's counter productive to repair a window and then throw a brick through it. What actions did you display this week that sabotaged your efforts to help your marriage?

WEEK FIVE ASSIGNMENT:

Married (1) Pray and ask God to help you keep from sabotaging your marriage with destructive words and actions. (2) In chapter 4's assignment you were to observe and write down the things your spouse cares about. This week act on what you wrote regarding what your spouse cares about. (3) Plan a vacation or mini vacation with your spouse.

Conclusion

It's Possible

An elderly man was looking out of his window
when he noticed a young boy throwing rocks.
He watched for several minutes in amazement before he eventually
went outside to approach the boy. He asked the young boy, "What
are you doing?" The boy replied, "I'm trying to hit something."
Confused the elderly man asked, "What do you mean something?
Do you not know what you are aiming to hit?" The boy paused,
and thought for a moment; then he replied, "I'm not completely
sure, but once I hit it, I'll know!"

What are you aiming for

I started this book by asking, what are your relationship goals? And we discovered many people start their relationships without fully knowing what they are aiming for. People know they want a *Happily Ever After* marriage, but getting there can be an aimless pursuit until you attempt to aim for your target.

SUCCESS IS HARD WORK, PERSEVERANCE, LEARNING, STUDYING, SACRIFICE, AND MOST OF ALL, LOVE OF WHAT YOU ARE DOING

~ PELE

My reason for writing this book was to help people build better relationships. I've had my share of bumps and bruises. I've seen enough people experience the same to know relationships aren't something you can aimlessly hope comes out for the best. Success is not an accident. It's something you must work at and build towards.

The principles laid out in this book are not only meant to be read, but applied. Learning about discipleship won't help you unless you take the time to follow the foundational principles. Having community to support and encourage you won't do you any good if you don't connect with your community. Data-collecting friendships won't happen if you rush into courtship and maintaining a healthy marriage only happens when you make sacrifices for your spouse.

As we learn new concepts, it takes time to implement them and break old habits. Most us have unhealthy habits in relationships and breaking them doesn't happen overnight. Be patient! At the end of each chapter there are questions and assignments designed for your benefit. They are meant to help you take the principles of this book and apply them for the purpose of building new habits. Take time to engage in the questions and weekly assignments. If you didn't do so while reading the book, go back to each chapter and follow the life application instructions.

Be mindful that each assignment is meant to be a *one-week* process. This will give you time to reflect and implement the principles shared. Regardless of whether you are single or married, each chapter has something for you! Once you've completed your week five assignment, go back and reread the current relationship phase you are in.

In some cases this may mean rereading more that one chapter. For example, if you are married and find yourself struggling with happiness or contentment, then rereading Chapter 2 will help you to better apply chapter five. Journal your thoughts and communicate your progress with your mentor or accountability partner. Above all, trust God, because happiness is possible.

Happiness is possible!

Do you expect your *Happily Ever After* to look like everyone else's? Do you think your path to getting there will be the same?

When you read about relationships in the Bible, you will find that all of them are different. Abraham and Sarah's marriage was different from Isaac and Rebekah's. Just as, Jacob and Rachel's path was different. Not every man was a Boaz and not every woman was a Ruth. Joseph thought about divorcing Mary the mother of Jesus, until divine intervention. Leah was unhappy until her fourth child when she finally sought contentment in God instead of in her husband. Paul was happily fulfilled, yet he remained unmarried. All of these stories are different. Their paths were different, yet they all shared a common thread, faith in God.

> Not every man was a Boaz and not every woman was a Ruth

Do you truly believe happiness is possible?

You cannot doubt what God wants to do in your life and expect to see it come true! Those who doubt are like those tossed To and Fro (Eph. 4:14)! Don't allow negative experiences to leave you cynical of relationships or the process. Even when you feel you are faced with the impossible, you must believe that God exist, and that He will reward you as you diligently seek Him (Heb. 11:6). I want to challenge you in closing to trust God.

TRUST GOD AND KNOW YOU CAN BE
HAPPY IN SINGLENESS.

TRUST GOD AND KNOW YOU CAN BE
HAPPY IN MARRIAGE.

TRUST GOD AND KNOW YOU CAN BE HAPPY.

Happiness isn't in someone else's story; your happiness is in your own!

Photo Credits

Page 2: "arrows & target" by i3alda via 123RF Stock Photo

Page 8: "house & blueprints" by franckito via 123RF Stock Photo

Pages 11, 25, 45, 71, 85: "construction stages" by Onyxprj via 123RF Stock Photo

Page 17: "balancing woman by retrorocket via 123RF Stock Photo

Page 36: "hands in stack" by William P via 123RF Stock Photo

Pages 47, 48, 49, 50, 62: "stick figures" by franckito via 123RF Stock Photo

NOTES

1. "Marriage & Divorce." American Psychological Association , 2018, www.apa.org/topics/divorce/.

2. "Statistics." American Sexual Health Association: Your Source For Sexual Health Information, 2018, www.ashasexualhealth.org/stdsstis/statistics/.

3. "Infidelity Statistics." Statistic Brain, 8 Sept. 2016, www.statisticbrain.com/infidelity-statistics/.

4. Smietana, Bob. "Americans Are Fond of the Bible, Don't Actually Read It." LifeWay Research, 23 Aug. 2017, lifewayresearch.com/2017/04/25/lifeway-research-americans-are-fond-of-the-bible-dont-actually-read-it/.

5. date. (n.d.). *Dictionary.com Unabridged.* Retrieved March 31, 2018 from Dictionary.com website http://www.dictionary.com/browse/date

6. Olson, Randy. "What Makes for a Stable Marriage?" Dr. Randal S. Olson, 7 Nov. 2014, www.randalolson.com/2014/10/10/whatmakes-for-a-stable-marriage/.

LISTEN WEEKLY TO PASTOR WALLACE

SimplifyComplexity.org

BrianEWallace.com

FOLLOW PASTOR BRIAN WALLACE

    @BrianEWallace

   *@BrianEWallace*1

Made in the USA
Lexington, KY
02 December 2019